TORN APART
THE PARTITION OF INDIA

For my dad

Published in the UK by Scholastic Children's Books, 2021
Euston House, 24 Eversholt Street, London, NW1 1DB
A division of Scholastic Limited

London ~ New York ~ Toronto ~ Sydney ~ Auckland
Mexico City ~ New Delhi ~ Hong Kong

Scholastic Ltd., Ireland Offices at: Unit 89E, Lagan Road,
Dublin Industrial Estate, Glasnevin, Dublin 11

ISBN 978-93-5471-007-0

A CIP catalogue record for this book is available from the British Library.

First edition: July 2021

This reprint edition: August 2023

Printed in India at MicroPrints India, New Delhi

www.scholastic.co.uk

SWAPNA HADDOW

TORN APART

THE PARTITION OF INDIA

USEFUL WORDS

ABBU: father in Urdu

AMMI: mother in Urdu

CHAI WALLAH: a person who sells and serves tea

JAAN: Urdu for 'loved one' or 'darling'

MAATA: mother in Hindi

AUGUST 1947

PROLOGUE

"The British Raj has ruled India since 1858," the headmaster's voiced boomed over the speakers as he addressed us from the podium. "But now they are leaving." He thrust a finger into the air. "India will have her independence!"

The entire student body erupted with roars of joy, and though the headmaster didn't tolerate rowdiness usually, he'd allowed us to shout out loud that one time. The blooms on the school lawn seemed to have blossomed especially in the orange, white and green colours of our nation's flag, nourished by the triumphant news. We felt alive with hope as we danced in the school yard with one another.

The headmaster hushed us quiet and spoke again. This time his voice was sombre.

"Children," he said. "Independence comes at a cost. The British have decided that India will be divided into two nations, India and Pakistan." The yard was silent. "I want you all to remember that no matter what happens to our motherland," he continued, "in this school, we are united."

In our excitement, we didn't stop to think about the inevitable changes to come. With the British leaving, the Indian leaders would form a new government. We didn't realize it then, celebrating together, but the India we knew and loved would be torn apart.

Soon after that assembly, the classrooms started to empty. First the British children left. Then the British teachers. Then the Muslims stopped coming. The headmaster called together the few of us who were left and explained that many of the Muslim staff and students had moved to Pakistan already. He said the New India wasn't for Muslims. And then he left too.

Abbu had laughed it all off at first and told me, "They will come back tomorrow. Just you see."

But the world had changed and they didn't come

back the next day. Nor the day after.

I knew it would be our turn to leave at some point, but I hadn't realized how soon.

OCTOBER 1947

CHAPTER 1

IBRAHIM

"*Ibrahim, hurry!*"

In the darkness, Ammi grabbed the blanket from my bed.

"Put this on," she said, shoving my shirt in my hands. "*Quickly!*"

The collar pulled against the back of my neck from the weight of the money Ammi had sewn into the lining the previous night. I grabbed my *topi* hat from the dresser and tucked it in my shirt pocket.

"Take your sister," Ammi whispered, pushing Nafia's tiny clammy hand into mine.

Blinking in the darkness, I pulled Nafia after me. I felt for the wall and then the doorway and stumbled out into the hall.

The marble floor was icy from the cold early morning air and I could feel Nafia pulling hard as she leaped back towards the bedroom.

"We have to go," I hissed at her, hauling her up on to my back. As she wrapped her arms around my shoulders and held on tight, I could smell the coconut oil Ammi put in her hair.

I followed the low growl of the car outside to where Abbu was lugging large trunks up on to its roof.

Abbu had explained it all last night. We had to leave Delhi. We were going to Pakistan. We had a private car. He and Ammi would pack, and I would get Nafia into the car quickly and quietly. That was my job.

"But why?" I had asked.

"Because it isn't safe here for us any more," answered Abbu.

"When will we come back?"

"We won't."

"But what about Suleiman and Faisal?"

"We don't have time to say goodbye to your friends."

"But I promised Faisal he could have my bike."

"You shouldn't make promises you can't keep, Ibrahim," Abbu had sighed, scolding me.

"Can I take the bike to him now?"

"No. It's not safe."

"Can I send them a letter to say where I've gone?"

"No."

"But why?"

"Because the world is changing," Abbu had shouted, slamming his hands down on the table between us. Ammi's sewing kit rattled and bobbins of white thread toppled over the edge and down the table legs. "This is independence, and independence means partition," he continued as he got to his feet. "And because I've told you already that we have to leave Delhi. We are going to Pakistan. We have a private car arriving very early. Ammi will pack and you need to get Nafia into the car quickly and quietly. *That* is your job."

He had stormed off to his office, signalling the end of the conversation.

"But why, Ammi?" I'd asked my mother. She'd wrung her hands and her glass bangles tinkled together. Then she hugged me close.

"This is a new India now," she said softly. "It's not *our* India any more."

We had sat in silence for a while before she too got up and left.

I stayed in the front room a while longer, stroking the soft fabric on Ammi's favourite chair and staring at the silk throw, trying to memorize the patterns that she had spent the past year embroidering. She'd created outlines, in tiny neat stitches of gold and silver, of kites and camels and horses and tiny dolls; all the things Nafia and I loved. And when we were ill or sad or had had a bad day at school, she would wrap us tightly in the special throw so we were swaddled by all the things that made us happy.

And now we would have to leave the silk throw behind, as we were forced out of our home with only a few of our possessions and memories of our time together in India.

We were leaving our home and Delhi under the cover of darkness. My chest felt tight, like a clamp being screwed harder and harder into the centre of my body. I balled my hands into fists, crushing Ammi's throw, and squeezed my eyes shut so tightly they stung. I knew in my heart we wouldn't be back tomorrow either, nor the day after, nor *any* day after that.

We have to leave Delhi. We are going to Pakistan. We have a private car. Abbu and Ammi will pack and I will get Nafia into the car quickly and quietly. That is my job. I repeated it over and over in my head like I was memorizing a poem to recite in class.

Abbu had already packed some cases into the back of the car when I helped Nafia in. It wasn't yet dawn and, in the darkness, the only light came from the car lamps, which lit up Abbu's worn face as he counted out wads of rupees for the driver.

"Where are we going?" Nafia asked with a yawn.

I held a finger to my lips and gave her the look Ammi gave me when she meant business.

Nafia squeezed her doll tightly and curled into a ball as I slid in next to her.

Abbu placed the last of our cases by the side of the car and Ammi came out to help him load them in next to us. I pulled my feet up as she pushed a case into the gap by my legs and climbed in after. Abbu grabbed the last trunk and heaved it high on to the roof of the car. It thudded into place on top of the others. The driver tossed a thick rope over the cases, tying them securely to the roof.

"Where are we going?" Nafia asked again, sleepily.

Ammi shushed her quiet and Nafia sat back in a sulk next to me as Abbu climbed into the front seat next to the driver.

He nodded at the driver and the car rumbled to life. As we took off, I looked back and watched our home being swallowed up into the night. It was the place where I had tossed a cricket ball for the first time, and many more times after that. Where Abbu had swung me so high I could touch the ceiling. Where Nafia had got trapped under the bed and Ammi and I had laughed so hard we had tears in our eyes as her podgy legs squirmed to freedom. It was the place where I was given my very first schoolbooks by Abbu, who was so proud of me as I paraded my schoolbag across the veranda.

I watched out of the window as we drove past my school, past the *chai wallah*, past the potters. The ladies who sold the jasmine garlands for the Hindu temple were not yet up and the moonlight shone upon the empty steps.

Ammi wept and Abbu turned to offer her his hand. She brushed it back and held her *dupatta* shawl up against her mouth to stifle her sobs. I sat still, unsure what to do. Ammi had never cried in front of me before.

Then the car stopped.

Ammi straightened up suddenly, and then went still. I couldn't see her face fully in the darkness. I twisted to see what was going on when the moonlight caught her face. I knew right then that I had to be the most silent I had ever been in my life.

That's when I heard it. The low muffle of voices followed by the slapping of sandals on the road. Quiet at first, then louder and louder. And closer. Faster and faster and faster.

The back window exploded as a rock smashed through, hitting Ammi in the shoulder. Nafia screamed as glass shards shattered on to the back seat. I could taste blood as thick drops trickled down the side of my face.

Ammi threw open the door. She grabbed me and I grabbed Nafia. We tore out of the car. My arm caught the door and I screamed as glass cut through my skin.

"Run!" Abbu yelled, as angry voices grew louder and louder.

They were shouting at us. They snatched the cases off the car. They ripped into them like a pack of hungry wolves.

Abbu seized a trunk. A man with a wooden bat smacked him in the back of his legs and my father crumbled to the ground.

"Abbu!" I screamed for him. "Abbu!"

"Run!" he shouted back.

Ammi gripped me and Nafia and ran, dragging us after her. She swung Nafia up into her arms and we fled, Nafia's screams ripping through the night air.

I felt the mob behind me, close, like a fire growing, raging and angry.

My legs burned but I willed them on faster.

As we turned the corner on to the next street, I suddenly felt Ammi being wrenched away from me. Our hands struggled to stay connected.

"Run!" she cried, as the group of men grabbed my arms, pulling me away from her.

"Ammi!" I screamed.

"Run, Ibrahim!" Ammi cried again as I saw her and Nafia run free from the mob and tear down the road on the opposite side of the street.

I pulled hard away from the men holding me, thrashing my arms and breaking free. I bolted, fleeing in the opposite direction, Ammi's terrified cries echoing in my head.

CHAPTER 2

AMAR

It was just after dawn at the station when I saw the boy on the platform. He looked so out of place.

It wasn't that he was the only Muslim there. There were plenty of others waiting to board the Pakistan Special, all trying to get out of Delhi. All trying to escape justice for what they had done to Gopi, my friend.

But I wasn't going to let them.

The boy fidgeted with his shirt, pulling at the neck as he looked every which way for the train to Lahore. He tried to loiter by a family eating mangoes but he clearly wasn't with them. Perhaps he thought he would be safer alongside them. The youngest of the mango eaters, a little girl, peeled the skin of the fruit off with her teeth. She sent sprays of yellow pulp down the front of her dress and wiped her sticky hands on her scarf. The boy noticed this too. I watched as he looked at her with concern, almost reaching over to protect her from her own mess, as though he was well-versed in looking after a younger sister.

I shook my head. No. I could not think about the boy or his own family. I could not let anything distract me from avenging my best friend's death.

But the boy's life story crept into my head like a vine, twisting its way through my brain and making roots I couldn't weed out. See, I'd been trained to read people. Gopi had taught me how to pick out the rich men and this boy stank of money.

He was probably the son of a businessman or a wealthy doctor. He probably slept in a bed of his own that sat on a marble floor and had a servant to pack up his schoolbooks and pens for him each night. His mother probably gave him warm milk before bed and told him stories of prophets and princes. She probably swept the hair off his forehead to kiss him goodnight and called him *jaan* before he slept soundly, dreaming peacefully, wrapped in cotton sheets as soft as clouds.

That's why he looked so out of place. He was the son of a rich man.

So, why was he here at Delhi station? And without his rich-man father?

I watched the boy as he slid in behind a new family and away from the messy mango eaters. But the woman shot him a dirty look and he cowered back to his original spot by the sticky little girl. The platform was filling up now. People packed in tight like thousands of ants on a single lump of sugar. The little girl disappeared into the crush, but I could still see the boy. He clutched his arm, protecting it from the growing crowds of people, jostling for space on the platform. There was a small red stain on his torn sleeve where blood had soaked through. He was hurt.

I looked at the scar on my own arm. I'd cut my arm the night I met Gopi. We'd been running from the night police and their *lathi* sticks. Gopi had climbed the clock tower at Chandni Chowk to escape them and I had followed after him. I'd caught my arm on an untethered steel rod and screamed out in pain, but Gopi had told me to stop crying. "Only little babies cry," he'd said. I was seven years old and I was a man now, he'd told me. My slashed arm was a war wound, something to be proud of, proof that the streets belonged to me and I didn't need anyone else.

From then on, Delhi was our playground. We adventured everywhere together, spotting rich men with thick wallets and sneaking swigs of tea from the finest *chai wallahs* in the city. We slept in the doorways of temples bedecked with garlands of flowers and dozed by the light of the *diya* lamps decorating the shrines before being chased away by the temple workers and their brooms.

We relied on the good nature of the Delhiites and the stupidity of the rich men and their fat wallets to live from one day to the next, and that suited us just fine.

That was until independence. Early that morning, Gopi and I had joined hundreds of others at the *chai wallah* to listen to the broadcast from All India Radio. There had been deafening roars of joy when the man on the radio announced that the British Raj had left and we were now free from their rule.

Orange, white and green flags, emblazoned with the Ashoka Chakra, were hoisted high on every building, fluttering in the wind like hands waving the British off Indian soil. The flag above the Lahori Gate of the Red Fort flew highest and could be seen for miles. A military parade was held at Rajpath. And thousands and thousands of people gathered in Princess Park to listen to Prime Minister Nehru talk about India's destiny.

Gopi and I ran from one party to the next. There had been dancing and singing in the streets. The temples were overflowing with well-wishers and I remember the smell of the vegetable oil in the lit *diyas* that burned all day and all night long. Even their tiny flames danced.

There had been women in the streets handing out colourful sweets to everyone who passed by. Gopi and I scampered back nearly fifty times to the lady to refill our bellies with *mithai* in all the colours of the Indian flag. And when we were eventually chased away, we grabbed huge handfuls of the soft coconut candies and climbed to the top of the clock tower where we feasted and watched over the market below.

That night, the sky was filled with fireworks and the sound of firecrackers. Lights showered across the darkness and Gopi and I stayed up all night, watching the rainbow explosions lighting up Delhi.

But then they announced a new border. And the new border made everyone angry. The firecrackers and lights turned to gunfire and blood.

It was less than two days before the fighting started in the streets near us. One night, as we sat in the clock tower, we could see flames rising on the horizon from the far side of the city. An entire neighbourhood was alight. Long angry flames rose high into the dark sky. So many miles away, we could see the burning and smell the smoke and we were sure that no one could have survived it.

We spent the next few weeks hiding in the gutters with stray dogs, away from the violence, but when it became too dangerous to be out in the open, we hid in the ruins of burned-down houses and behind barricades of looted horse carts. The Muslims slaughtered the Hindus. The Hindus murdered the Muslims. The revenge killings grew and grew like an out-of-control forest fire.

The rich men left. And so did their fat wallets. The women in the streets with their *mithai* never returned. There was no more dancing. There was no more singing.

Gopi and I took turns sleeping. On those nights when our eyelids grew too heavy, we would wake to the bitter smell of gunpowder and charred rubber. And just when we thought the gunfire had stopped, it started again like hail, cracking through the sky.

Then the looters came. They took everything.

And they took my Gopi's life.

I felt in my pocket for the rocks I had sharpened. I restringed my slingshot catapult and loaded it, holding it up and taking aim.

The Muslim boy was still in my sights.

He stood there in his rich clothes. He didn't care about what had happened to Gopi, but I would make him.

I could hear the blood pounding in my ears. I

shook my head, trying to get rid of the sound. I pulled back on the elastic, readjusting my aim again.

I had to concentrate on the boy.

The ground beneath me started to rumble, rocking me off the rails. I dropped my catapult as a train thundered into the station and pulled up against the platform.

I was used to seeing trains come and go from the station, bursting with travellers. But this train was different.

There were no crowds of people with their trunks stacked high on the roofs. There were no heads poking out of the carriages or between the buffers. There were no arms and legs hanging out of the windows. And there were no excited noisy children perched in the doors.

The driver shut off the engine and the station master pulled open a carriage door. And everything was still.

CHAPTER 3

IBRAHIM

The crowd of people on the platform heaved forwards, pulling out tickets and waving them in the air. I realized I didn't have one. I edged back but was pushed forwards as a new wave of people joined the crowd. Every sharp elbow I knocked against sent pain shooting through my body from where I had sliced my arm.

People were yelling and shoving and I gave in to

the drag of the crowd. I looked up at the train as I was thrust sideways. Scrawled on the side of the train in blood were the words "a present from Pakistan".

And then the bodies of the Hindu refugees fell out.

Vomit rose in my throat, gagging me. And then the screaming started. I could hear the guards on the track yelling at us to get back. And then I saw men with knives push across the platform. They waved their weapons high, like the travellers had done with their tickets only a moment ago. The sounds were nightmarish as they started attacking the Muslim crowd on the platform.

A woman pulled me back behind her and held her hands over my ears but I could still hear the Hindu men on the platform screaming that no Muslim would be spared.

A man fell down next to us. His leg had been slashed. Another fell on top of him, crushing him in the stampede as people ran to get away.

I broke free from the woman and jumped down on to the tracks. I had to get away. I turned back to the platform for a moment. People were clambering over each other like they were bricks on the floor.

My stomach heaved and I choked down the vomit. I had no time to think. I quickly broke away from the other Muslim travellers on the platform. A group of Hindu men armed with knives and sticks started running after me. I had to get out of there. I fled across the tracks towards the empty train carriages parked ahead.

There was a boy with a slingshot catapult. I hurtled towards him.

"Help me," I cried.

He stared at me.

I pulled on his arm and a rock dropped from his hand.

"Help me," I begged again.

He looked at me and looked up at the pack coming towards me. Then he ran.

I chased after him.

"Go away!" he yelled at me.

"You have to help me!" I yelled back at him.

A rock hit my back as I ran. My feet slipped out from under me. I fell forwards over the track. A rain of stones pelted my head as I pushed up on my grazed hands and launched forwards. The boy ran on ahead of me. I careered after him, willing my legs to pump faster and faster.

My lungs were on fire. The men were close behind. Sweat streamed into my eyes, stinging and blurring my vision. I wiped my eyes hard with the back of my hand and ran on. My hands in tight fists, I pushed harder, outrunning the men who were weighed down with their heavy wooden bats and iron rods.

I caught sight of the boy. He ran across the tracks going in the opposite direction and clambered up a wall back into the city.

I ran at the wall and hurled myself up, gripping the edge with the tips of my fingers and swinging my legs up and over before falling to the ground on the other side.

The boy sprang up from behind an overturned barrel barricade. He looked at me, bewildered.

"Why did you leave me?" I shouted at him.

"Why are you following me?" he roared back, stepping forwards and looming over me.

I got to my feet. Every part of my body seared with pain.

"Why didn't you help—" I shouted again, glaring

at the boy. But he pressed his hand over my mouth and pointed to his ear. The slap of shoes on dirt was coming closer towards the other side of the wall. He seized my arm and we sprinted towards the crowded road.

Before we hit the crowd, he pulled me into an empty alley. He pushed me towards an abandoned horse cart and tapped the edge before cupping his hands together low to give me a leg up on to the cart. He clambered up after me and hauled himself up through a glassless window frame into a deserted building.

The sound of running men was getting closer and closer. After a second the boy stuck his head out through the window and reached out his hand to help me up. He tugged hard and my shoulder clicked out of place. I screamed out in pain but he kept pulling and pulling until he dragged me in through the window frame.

"Quiet," he hissed as I cowered low beneath the window, holding my arm close.

CHAPTER 4

AMAR

Why couldn't I do it?

I'd seen the boy coming towards me. I'd taken aim. I was ready. I was ready to avenge Gopi. But when he looked me in the eye and said, "Help me!" my chest felt tight and my hands wouldn't move.

The boy was following me like my own shadow. I could hear the men in the street below. The boy was groaning and trembling. His arm hung out of its socket, dangling like a broken twig. If he screamed, he would get us both killed.

"Give me that," I whispered, grabbing for his *topi*, poking out of his shirt pocket.

"What are you doing?" he cried, arching away from me.

"Shhhh," I hissed at him. I jabbed my finger at the window where the men were lurking beneath.

"What are you doing?" he hissed back between shallow breaths, pushing me away.

"You want to get rid of that mob, don't you?"

He nodded.

I held out my hand and he reluctantly passed me his *topi*. I took the hat and pulled up the sleeve of his injured arm. Blood was still oozing from the wound I had seen earlier. I rubbed the hat against the cut.

"What are you doing?" he whimpered again.

"Trust me," I whispered back.

The dark blood stained the hat.

"Wait here," I whispered. "And stay quiet."

The men with their weapons were outside searching the gutters in the road.

I whistled for their attention. "What are you looking for?"

"Nothing that concerns you," one of them sneered, looking up at me. "Get out of here."

"Wait," said the one with the moustache, his upper lip curled in a snarl. "He might have seen the Muslim boy."

"Yeah, I saw him," I said. I tossed the boy's *topi* down to them. "And that's what's left of him now."

The one with the moustache picked it up and examined the blood. He gave me a small smile and nodded his head at the others, calling them to follow him back out to the main road. I watched them leave from the window and didn't drop back down by the boy until I was sure they were long gone.

"Now they think you're dead, they won't come looking for you," I told the boy.

I sat down, crouched beneath the window. The boy had stopped whimpering but he was still trembling. His eyes were shut and his breathing was fast and shallow.

I remembered a time when Gopi was ill. His skin was clammy and his breathing fast. He couldn't stand;

his legs were too weak to carry his skinny body. He told me he had a fever and I knew he needed help. For the first time, living on the streets, I was scared. Of course, no hospital wanted to deal with the street children like us so I carried Gopi back across the city on my back, to our home under the bridge. I stayed up all night wiping away the sweat from his face with my shirt as he moaned and writhed. By the morning he was able to sit up. He wanted water, and when he was able to stand up again, he wanted food.

The boy would need the same too.

I got up and looked around the building. It had been a tailor's shop before it had been surrendered to the looters. I gathered up some fabric from a cutting table. I searched down the narrow corridor at the back and found a door, which opened into a bathroom with a bucket in one corner and a sink in the other. I twisted the sink tap. It gurgled and spluttered but nothing flowed. The bucket was half filled with water so I took that instead.

When I returned, the boy was awake and sat back with a start when I came towards him, as though he had forgotten my face for a moment.

"I have water," I said, placing the bucket down next to him.

His eyes narrowed as he squinted up at me and then down into the bucket. He dipped his hand in the water and wet his face.

"The men outside?" he asked.

"They've gone," I reassured him.

He nodded as though to reassure himself too. "Thank you."

He scooped up more water and wiped his face again.

"My shoulder is dislocated," the boy said quietly. "Can you help me click it back into place?"

His arm sagged by his side at an awkward angle, and he winced as he turned to show me.

"I don't know how," I said.

"It's okay. I saw my father fix our neighbour's shoulder after he fell from a ladder. I'll talk you through it," he said, shuffling around to face me. "It's just basic anatomy."

He pointed to the fabrics and I handed them to him. He searched through them, like he was selecting a sari for a new bride. He took a small section and wrapped the bleeding gash on his arm before choosing a larger triangular cut-off and handing it to me.

"You will need to tie this round my neck and across my arm like a sling after you fix my shoulder," he said, using his uninjured arm to show me where to put it. He knelt up on his knees. "Come and sit opposite me," he said.

I did as he said and he shuffled closer to me.

"Put your hand on my shoulder," he said.

I swallowed and took a breath, gently placing my hand on his shoulder.

"Now take my wrist and guide my shoulder back into the socket," the boy continued, his jaw clenched tightly because of the pain. "You will need to twist my arm a bit to make sure you get it in right."

I held his shoulder more firmly. He flinched and shrank back.

"Should I stop?" I asked, hesitant.

"No, no. . ." he stuttered. "Pass me that piece of wood," he said, pointing to a broken ruler behind me.

He slid the ruler into his mouth and bit down, and then nodded at me to reach for his shoulder again before he squeezed his eyes shut.

He let out a strangled growl, biting hard on the ruler as I twisted his arm. The bones crunched as they slipped back into place. I grabbed the fabric quickly and tied his arm.

"Thank you," he whispered.

"You're welcome," I said, collapsing back next to him.

"I'm Ibrahim," he said.

"I'm Amar," I said back.

CHAPTER 5

IBRAHIM

Amar pulled at the neck of his *kurta* shirt, which was brown with dust and wear. His toes curled over the edges of his torn slippers. He looked like he was the same age as me – maybe he was eleven too or perhaps even twelve – but his body was so skinny that when he squatted to sit down, his kneecaps jutted against his skin like oversized books in a small cloth bag.

He had clearly been living rough on the streets for most of his life, if not all of it.

I had to look away as I thought guiltily about the way Ammi would grip mine and Nafia's hands tight and yank us away to the other side of the road when we saw street children. "Don't look at the beggars," she would say, as though living on the streets was something we could catch like a cold.

Amar caught me staring at him again and I glanced away quickly, pretending to explore the looted store from where I was sitting.

"Do you live here?" I asked, breaking the silence.

"No," he said, shaking his head.

"Where's your family?" I asked.

He said nothing and I wasn't sure if he'd understood what I'd said.

"Your mother?" I said slowly. "Where is your mother? Where is your father?"

He glared at me. "Why are you talking so slowly?" he retorted. "Do you think I'm stupid because I don't wear your fancy clothes?" He stared down at my shoes and suddenly I felt ashamed for judging him.

My face burned hot as I stammered to answer him

back. "No, no, no. Not at all." I pulled my feet in under me. "These old shoes are worthless anyway; they were hand-me-downs from my cousin," I said, making up a story to play down my wealth.

"Then give them to me," he said calmly.

"What?"

"Give me your shoes if you think they're worthless."

"Oh, okay," I said, confused, pulling off my shoes, not quite sure what I was now agreeing to.

He took off his own broken shoes, pulled on mine and then jumped up, tapping his feet on the floor. "Can I keep them?" he asked.

"Errr," I started, looking at my own bare feet. "I don't actually have a spare pair on me."

He nodded his head like that was my permission for him to keep them, and he continued to beat his feet hard on the floor.

For a moment I considered asking for my shoes back, but then I remembered that Amar had saved my life. The least I could do was let him have my shoes.

"Your family?" I asked again. "Where are they?"

"What family?" He shrugged.

I swallowed hard. "Sorry."

"It's okay," he said quickly. "Where is *your* family?"

My chest ached as I thought back to earlier that morning. "We were heading to Pakistan when we became separated during an attack."

"Were they at the train station too?" he asked.

"No," I said. "I don't know where they are."

I pushed up off the wall, careful of my arm, and got to my feet.

Amar kicked over his broken slippers to me. "You can have those if you want," he offered.

Not wanting to offend him, I cautiously slipped my feet into the worn sandals. They were surprisingly comfortable, cushioned and warm from all the wear, but I knew when I next saw Ammi there was no way I could tell her about this exchange.

"Thank you," I said.

"You need to be careful out there," he said, walking towards the front of the shop. "Good luck finding your family."

"Wait," I called after him. "Where are you going?"

"I don't know." He shrugged again and kicked at the store receipts strewn across the floor as he walked on.

I followed after him. Amar didn't stop. Instead he continued to walk through the shop, this time a little faster.

I walked a little faster too, holding my bandaged arm in place.

"Why are you always following me?" he demanded, stopping so suddenly I almost fell over him.

"I thought we were going somewhere," I replied, taken aback.

"*I'm* going somewhere," he said. "And *you're* going somewhere else."

"But I don't know where I am," I admitted. "I don't know this part of Delhi."

"Look," he said, staring me straight in the face. "I could be killed for protecting you. It's just best if we part ways now."

He was right. He had risked his life helping me. The Hindu gangs would just as easily see him as dead as me if they knew he had helped a Muslim.

As he spun to leave, a slingshot catapult fell from his pocket. I reached down to pick it up.

"Did you make this yourself?" I asked, admiring the whittled wood. "It's really good."

He snatched it back, unable to meet my eye and shoved it into his waistband. And then he stopped and looked me up and down, shaking his head.

"You can't go out there like that," he sighed.

He searched through the shelves, hauling up fabrics and pushing through the piles of textiles. All the sewing machines had been taken but there were rolls of thread and wooden bobbins. My chest tightened again as thoughts of Ammi and her embroidered silk came flooding back. Where was she? Was she safe? Was she still with Nafia, and had Abbu found them?

"Wear this," he said, thrusting a *kurta* shirt towards me.

"I'm okay in this," I said, tucking my shirt into my trousers and placing a hand over the secret compartment of cash.

"You'll be dead in a minute looking like that," he said. He peeked out at the street through a smashed windowpane. "This is a Hindu neighbourhood and nobody wears a uniform like that."

I looked down at my smart shirt and trousers. Ammi had wanted to make a good impression when we arrived in Pakistan. But Amar was right. I would better disguised in a *kurta*.

"Where do I pay for this?" I asked, lifting up the *kurta* tentatively.

He laughed, smacking his forehead with his palm. "Do you see a teller around here?"

"I can't just take it!" I exclaimed. "That's stealing."

He stared at me like I had sprouted three horns. "It's not stealing. It's called surviving."

"Fine," I said. "Don't look."

He turned his back to me and I slid off my top. I unpicked the stitches Ammi had used to secure the money into the lining. I took out ten rupees and left it as payment on what remained of the smashed counter before folding up the rest of the cash and putting it in the *kurta* pocket. I pinned the pocket shut and slid the shirt over my head. I managed to get into one side but the shirt got caught up over my bandaged arm.

"Could you give me a hand?" I called to Amar.

He sighed but came to my aid. He removed the sling and helped me slide the *kurta* over my arm before retying the sling. I caught a glimpse of us in a shattered mirror. In our *kurtas*, we could've easily been mistaken for brothers.

But I had a family of my own. I needed to find Ammi and Abbu and Nafia. I had to get to the border. That was where we were heading. If I got to Pakistan, I could find them.

"Amar," I said. "I need to get to the border. Can you help me?"

"I have no idea where the border is," he scoffed. "And why would I help you? I don't want any trouble."

"I don't have anyone else," I pleaded.

"Well, I've never had anyone or anything my whole life," he said, pulling out the insides of his empty pockets.

The homemade catapult fell out from the back of Amar's waistband. I reached to pick it up for him again but he snatched it out of my grasp.

He stepped back from me and stood stiffly, suddenly unable to meet my eye. Seeing him with the catapult in his hand again pulled me back to the moment I'd pleaded with him for help at the train station. There he was, armed with a catapult in front of me as a mob of men armed with iron rods closed in.

My legs started to shake. I leaned back against the broken counter to steady myself, taking in deep breaths before I spoke.

"The catapult," I said quietly. "You had it at the station."

"So?" he said, his face flushing red as he whipped his hand behind his back.

"Why?"

"It's none of your business," he retorted.

We stood in silence, a heavy awkwardness hanging between us. I felt very aware of the ticking clock on the wall that hadn't been wrecked in the looting.

Tick. Tick. Tick. Tick.

Tick.

Tick.

"I needed to protect myself," Amar blurted out defensively, breaking the silence.

"Okay."

"Sometimes you need to settle a score, you know?" he muttered, shaking his head.

Tick. Tick. Tick.

"I had to do something," he murmured into his chest.

Like pieces of a puzzle clicking into place, I realized what it was that Amar was saying.

"You were at the station to hurt someone today, weren't you?" I said.

His shoulders drooped and his chin trembled.

The room started to spin in and out of focus. "Was I that someone?" I whispered.

Amar's shoulders shook.

I felt the acid in my stomach rise up into my throat and I choked on its taste. I slumped back against the counter and Amar stepped forwards to hold me upright.

"Sit down," he said.

I snatched my hand back quickly. "You were going to kill *me*?" I said incredulously.

"I didn't go through with it, did I?" he said defensively.

"What have I ever done to you?" I cried.

"You're a Muslim," he said quietly. "And my only friend in the world is dead because of you lot."

I took a breath. "*I* didn't kill your friend though."

"I know," he muttered through gritted teeth, dropping his head into his hands. "I'm sorry."

The room spun back into focus. He sounded genuine. He didn't look up. It was as though the guilt he felt hung from his head like a heavy weight, refusing to let him move.

With his head down, he spoke softly. "I really am sorry for being at the station for the reason I was."

"I'm sorry about what happened to your friend," I replied.

He took a moment. He slowly looked up and nodded. And then he backed away, ready to leave.

"But this means you owe me," I called after him.

"What?" he said, turning to face me again.

"You owe me. I can't get out of this neighbourhood without your help."

"I saved your life, didn't I?" he bargained.

"But you *were* planning to kill me!"

"Okay, okay," he said, throwing his hands up. "What do you want?"

"I need you to get me to the border," I demanded.

"No," he said, shaking his head. "Absolutely not. And even if I agreed, I don't even know where the border is."

"You can figure it out. You must know the whole

of Delhi," I said. "If anyone knows a way out of this city, it's you."

"I can't help you," he said, backing away. "It's too dangerous."

"I have money," I pleaded. "I have lots of money and you can have it. All of it."

He turned around on his heel. This time, I had his attention.

"The money is all yours if you get me to the border," I promised.

CHAPTER 6

AMAR

The wad of cash in Ibrahim's hand was the most money I had ever seen in my life. The notes were beautifully crisp, like they had just been printed straight into his palm.

"All of it?" I asked, suspicious.

"All of it," Ibrahim agreed, nodding. "But only after you get me to the border."

I hesitated. I didn't want any trouble and helping

Ibrahim would get me in a lot of trouble, but then again, I had never had this much money in my life.

"Okay," I said. "I'll get you to the border."

His eyes lit up and for a moment it felt like I was with Gopi again, his face delighted at finding an entire basket of mangoes.

"Thank you, thank you, thank you!" Ibrahim sang over and over and over.

"Okay, okay!" I laughed. "First, we need to get some food and find somewhere to hide."

"Can't we stay here?" he said, looking around.

I shook my head. "It's quiet now but by the evening the mobs will be out and things will get violent. We need to move somewhere safer whilst your arm recovers."

He nodded in agreement and we both looked at his stomach as it growled hungrily.

I looked back out at the road. There were a few people searching through the trashed, blackened shops, collecting discarded bits of steel and wood. A group of ladies covered in dust consoled a woman who wept into the folds of her sari. She held a faded photo in her hands. Another day, another death. Gopi's face popped into my head before being engulfed by a wave of aching as I was reminded I would never see him again. I squeezed my eyes shut, trying hard to quash the tearing pain in my chest.

Ibrahim, who couldn't see outside into the street, was bright-eyed and ready to get going. He bobbed up and down, like a little boy heading off on an adventure. I shielded his view of the ladies; I didn't want him to lose his nerve as we headed out into the street.

This would be our first test.

I cleared my throat. "This is a Hindu neighbourhood," I reminded Ibrahim, putting Gopi out of my mind. "You should only speak in Hindi."

He nodded eagerly.

"And do something with your hair," I said.

"What's wrong with my hair?" he said, looking surprised.

"You look like you have money, like you can afford for someone to cut your hair," I said. "You might as well put a target on your back that says, 'I have money, please rob me'."

I reached up to his pruned head and rubbed my hand through it, twisting it into a messy heap. I then scooped up a handful of soot from the floor and rubbed it over his *kurta*.

"Just keep your head down and try not to catch anyone's eye," I said, moving towards the door.

Ibrahim trailed after me, limping slightly.

"Did you hurt your leg too?" I asked, looking at his foot.

"No," he said. "I'm trying to blend in."

"Blend in with what?" I exclaimed. "All the limping Hindus around here?"

"I was just trying to get into character," he said defensively.

"And what character is that exactly?" I laughed. "A pirate with a wooden leg?"

"The character of someone who doesn't want a target on their back that says, 'I have money, please rob me'."

"Right," I said, shaking my head in despair. "Well, now you have a target on your back that says, 'I have money *and* a fake limp, please rob me'."

I stifled another snort of laughter as Ibrahim shot me the look of a wounded baby deer. He really *did* need my help.

"You will be fine," I reassured him. "Just walk like a normal person and try not to draw any attention to yourself."

I cracked open the shop door and peered out. The sunlight blinded me for a second, but then as my eyes adjusted, I saw the coast was clear. We slipped out on to the street, stepping over the glass and wooden splinters covering the paving in front. We passed the group of ladies in their saris who didn't give us a second glance. We overtook two men scavenging in the gutted shop fronts for metal to weld who said nothing. We even made it past an Indian soldier who let us walk by unquestioned. The thing about street children was that we had the ability to be invisible. Nobody wanted to see us so nobody did.

Ibrahim stayed close, but as we turned towards the market, he stopped. It was like he'd never seen Delhi before.

"Have you never been to a market?" I asked as we merged into the crowds of shoppers.

"Not really," he admitted. "The servants usually went for us."

"Servants?"

He blushed.

"How many servants did you have?"

"I don't know," he mumbled into his chest. "Ammi dealt with them."

His cheeks glowed a deep red whenever we spoke about his fancy haircuts, his expensive shoes or his servants.

"What is the most expensive thing you ever bought?" I asked, unable to resist.

His face turned even redder. "Do we have to talk about this?"

"What's wrong?"

"I thought I was not meant to be drawing attention to me having money," he said out of the side of his mouth, his eyes darting from left to right as though spies were following us.

"Okay, okay," I said, throwing up my hands.

We continued on through the market, past the *chai wallah* and the potter, and past the rows of begging street children. Gopi had saved me from that life. I wondered, if he could see me now, what he would say about me saving Ibrahim.

"Ammi once bought a *salwar kameez* suit that was covered in crystals and gold thread," Ibrahim said suddenly. "It was made of thick pink silk and took two months for the tailors to finish. Abbu said it was the most expensive thing in the house. He said once that it even cost more than a house," he continued, a small smile stretching wider across his face as he spoke. "Only, in that two months whilst it was being sewn, Ammi grew very fond of the *mithai* the cook bought from the sweetmeats shop, and when the *salwar kameez* finally arrived it was so tight she couldn't sit down, so she never actually wore it." He giggled and pretended to sit down without bending in the middle.

I tried too and soon we were laughing so hard a crowd of street children were pointing us in the direction of the nearest gutter because we looked like we were in urgent need of the toilet.

I called one of the street children over and told him to get us two plates of food and two teas from the *chai wallah*. Ibrahim passed him five rupees even though I told him that was far too much.

"That child can keep the rest," he said.

"You know that money will only go to the people that own him. He won't ever get to see one single rupee."

"How do you know?" Ibrahim asked as our food arrived.

"Because *I* was that street child once," I said. I scooped up a handful of *daal* and rice, balling it in my fingers and eating quickly. Ibrahim had stopped eating, unable to meet my eye.

"It's okay," I said, waving him to eat up. "You starving yourself won't help me or that child."

He reluctantly shovelled up some food and ate. His stomach growled again and he began to eat more hastily. He was so hungry he ordered a second plate, and I helped myself to another too.

We sat cross-legged, watching the people mill about the market. It wasn't as crowded as it usually was and people kept their heads down, making quick purchases before rushing away. There was a nervous energy over Chandni Chowk, the air so brittle it could snap at any moment.

Before it turned dark, I took Ibrahim to the clock tower. It would be safe there, at least for the night.

We climbed up the scaffolding slowly to the top, just in time to watch the sun set over Delhi.

Exhausted, we collapsed into a small crawl space, hidden away from the mobs and the guards and the looters.

"Thank you." Ibrahim sighed, falling asleep almost instantly, his head in my lap.

CHAPTER 7

IBRAHIM

As soon as I closed my eyes, my dreams were filled with Ammi's face. I could see Abbu and Nafia too and we were playing in our house. Ammi and I were hiding, waiting for Abbu to find us. Nafia had already jumped out of her hiding spot because her giggles had given her away. Abbu pretended to search high and low for us, feigning loud frustrated stomps around the house, and both

Ammi and I covered our mouths to stop us from laughing out loud.

And then the dream changed. I was back by the car. The dark was suffocating me as though someone had placed a tight sack over my head and was pulling it hard around my neck. Then I was running but I couldn't see where to go next. I heard Nafia screaming and I felt myself being pulled away from Ammi.

And then I woke up, just as I was about to be caught, as though my mind wouldn't let me go back to when we were separated.

All I could think about now was getting back to them.

Every part of my body ached as I struggled to sit upright. I was scared to reposition my arm to check how much movement I had, but at least now my shoulder sat more in line with its socket. It was the cut on my arm from the car that was worrying me the most. Blood and thick yellow pus had crusted my shirt sleeve where the bandage had soaked through overnight.

I looked over at Amar. He was still asleep on the hard floor, snoring gently. He had placed a sheet of cardboard over me to keep me warm during the night and I could see the goosebumps on his legs where he had slept in the cold.

I placed the cardboard over him, careful not to wake him. The sun was up and I could hear the early din of stalls being set up and the cries of a vendor passing below, selling his wares.

I arched my neck to see over the side of the clock tower. People setting up the market had stopped to crowd around the remains of a burning car.

Amar stirred so I sat back so as not to disturb him. My stomach growled and I wondered what Ammi, Abbu and Nafia were having for breakfast. I imagined them safely in Pakistan, perhaps in a hotel, eating egg curry and *roti*. Nafia would be drinking the remains of Abbu's tea as he read the paper looking for news of me. I wish I was sat at that table eating egg curry too.

"Can you control that sound?" Amar yawned as he nodded down at my stomach. "There are riots that are quieter than that growling."

"Sorry," I apologized, trying to grip my stomach into silence.

He sat up and pulled my injured arm towards him.

He gently pulled up my sleeve. The skin around the cut was greying and it felt numb as I prodded it.

"This doesn't look good," he said, looking concerned. He turned my arm over and back again, examining the gash. "You need to rest and your arm needs to heal," he said. "I don't know how long it will take us to reach the border so let's get out of the city centre and eat before we start the journey. It will be safer that way."

My face must have given away how scared I was feeling as I peered down at my arm, because he then said, "It's a war wound, something to be proud of, proof that the streets belong to you."

He tore the bottom of his *kurta* and used the fabric to wrap the weeping wound tight.

"What happened there?" I asked, changing the subject to take my mind off my arm. I pointed down at the market where more people had gathered now to look at the burning car.

"You slept right through a riot last night," Amar said.

I felt the blood drain from my face and I shut my eyes. I was back in the suffocating darkness again.

Amar sat straight up and looked at me. "Are you okay?"

I swallowed hard, trying to wet my sawdust-dry throat. "Yes," I choked. "Did you see what happened?"

"Sort of," he said, stretching his arms behind his back. "There were a group of men in the car and they were attacked."

"Are they okay?"

"I don't know," he replied, his face not giving away any emotion. "But they got out before the car was set alight so that was something at least."

My heart was thundering in my chest. "Do you know if they were Muslims or Hindus?"

Amar shrugged indifferently.

"I bet it was Muslims," I said. "Hindus aren't being kicked out of Delhi."

Amar rolled his eyes.

"Don't you even care that those people in the car might be dead?" I demanded to know. "How would they have made it out of Delhi without their car?"

Amar's blank look enraged me.

"Maybe you don't care because they were Muslims?" I taunted, hoping to see a flash of compassion in his eyes.

That group of men were like my family and me only yesterday, trying desperately to escape the danger in Delhi.

Amar sighed loudly, crossing his arms in front of him.

"Why are the mobs even out at night? What about the curfew?" I stated matter-of-factly. "Abbu told me the curfew keeps Delhi safe at night."

"What curfew?" Amar scoffed. "There's no curfew. Whilst you were sleeping tight in your palace with your servants, we were dealing with gangs with their iron rods and knives. And by the way, Hindus are being killed too." He got to his feet before continuing, "I do care. I care a lot in fact. I love Delhi and I hate what is happening but I can't get upset every time I see something happen. I need to survive too. If I thought of all the dead bodies I have seen in the last few months, it would be too much for me to bear."

He kicked at the floor with his foot.

My cheeks burned red. I'd never seen a dead body until yesterday at the train station. And just thinking back for a moment made me want to retch. I couldn't even imagine what Amar had seen in his life and the hardship he had endured.

The words I'd just said replayed over and over in my head, somehow sounding even more foolish each time. I'd been protected for so long, and only because I had been born to *my* ammi and *my* abba and not into a life like Amar's.

I felt ashamed by what I had said and I had the overwhelming desire for the clock tower to collapse and bury me alive.

"I'm sorry," I whispered with hot tears in my eyes.

"Good," Amar said. "You should be."

He reached out his hand and pulled me up. "We need to go before the police see us up here."

As we climbed down the scaffolding on the clock tower, I thought back to the train station. Amar was right. If I shut my eyes, I could smell the blood and hear the screams. It wasn't fair of me to say that Amar didn't care. He had walls up to protect himself and now I did too. Ammi, Abbu and Nafia's faces helped me to block out what had happened.

"Amar, I didn't mean to upset you," I said, breaking the silence.

"It's okay," he said. "I never take disagreements on an empty stomach seriously. That's just the hunger talking."

"I *am* hungry," I admitted, my stomach growling right on cue.

When we reached the bottom of the tower, I looked at the market and pointed to where we had eaten yesterday. "Can we go eat there again?" I asked keenly. "I have money."

"No!" he said. "That's *my* money remember and *I* decide when it's spent."

My face fell and my stomach roared angrily at Amar.

He grinned at me. "Don't worry, hungry tummy. I know where we can get the best mangoes in Delhi."

Amar took us west, heading away from the bustle and crowds.

"You know, some of my neighbours were Hindu," I said, as we hurried across Delhi. "We used to go to their houses for Diwali and share *mithai* and light firecrackers."

He smiled. "I loved Eid in Delhi. Me and my friend Gopi would watch the prayers from early in the morning at Jama Masjid and then we would be invited to eat at the shared meal in the bazaar." He pointed back towards the market. "This used to be a place where Muslims and Hindus all shopped side by side," he said sadly, and I saw that what was happening to India was hurting him as much as it was hurting me.

We continued at a pace, heading further and further from the city centre. The sky rumbled overhead before the swollen dark clouds broke. Rain pelted down hard and we rushed for cover, trying not to get soaked.

"This way!" Amar shouted over the storm.

He pointed towards a shelter in a hollow under a tree and I waited there as he ran off into the October showers on the hunt for mangoes.

I must have dozed off against the trunk of the tree because the slap of Amar splashing through muddy puddles startled me awake. He was hurrying towards me with a dozen mangoes cradled in the front of his *kurta*.

The first bite into the juicy yellow flesh was heavenly, like a first meal after a year without food.

"These *are* the best mangoes I've ever had!" I exclaimed.

"I told you," Amar replied smugly.

We sat in happy silence eating our way through the pile of mangoes. Once I was done, I held my sticky hands up into the rain and then wiped them down on my shirt.

Amar did the same and then pulled out a piece of notepaper from his shirt pocket and slowly unfolded it. Although it had browned over time and the folds in the paper had darkened into almost solid black lines, I could see this was something Amar had kept very safe.

"You can read, right?" he asked.

"Yes." I nodded.

He cleared his throat, as though he was embarrassed to ask me something. I peered at the notepaper in Amar's hands and I could see writing. He looked at the words as though they were just scribbles. I realized then that Amar couldn't do what I had taken for granted for so long. He couldn't read.

"It's okay," I said softly, holding out my hand. "Pass it to me."

"Can you read this?" he asked, unfolding the fragile paper carefully and placing it in my hand.

I scanned the writing and nodded again. "It looks like it's in Hindi," I explained. "Who is it from?"

He paused.

"I don't know," he said finally. He hesitated for a moment before saying, "It was with me when I was found at the Gauri Shankar Temple as a baby."

I looked at the paper carefully and read:

My darling son,

I am sorry.

May Lord Shiva watch over you.

Your maata.

"Mother," he repeated, the word barely audible.

I felt like I was snooping on a private moment as I watched him stare at the words on the paper, all the swirls of the alphabet finally making sense to him.

"You see this word here?" I said, pointing my finger to the end of the note. "That says '*maata*'."

Amar traced his finger over the letters. He then slowly copied them out in the dirt in front of us.

"*Maata*?" he said, looking up at me.

"Almost," I said, correcting the last letter.

He ran his finger in the dirt again. As the letters

filled with rainwater like tiny moats, he looked back at me again.

"That's right," I encouraged. "You've got it."

He clutched the note to his chest, hugging it so tight as though it was his mother.

"Can you teach me to read every word in this note?" he asked, wiping away the tears rolling down his cheeks.

"Of course," I said.

We continued to sit under the tree, our backs against its trunk as I read the note over and over again to him. Amar leaned his head back, his eyes closed tight, listening intently to every syllable of each word.

The rain started to ease and the tips of the grass twitched as the last of the tiny raindrops ran down into the earth. We sat in an easy silence as Amar thought of his *maata* and I thought of Ammi, both of us longing to be with them in that moment.

"I met Gopi at the Gauri Shankar Temple," Amar said suddenly.

"Your friend who died?" I asked.

He nodded. "I was trying to find a place to sleep so I went to the temple and he was there too."

He smiled, thinking fondly of his friend.

"What happened to Gopi?" I asked.

Amar looked away, but not before I saw the tears well in his eyes. All at once, I was weighed down by the heaviness he had in his heart over the loss of his friend. It was hard to breathe.

I reached out my hand and squeezed his shoulder as he leaned back and shut his eyes, remembering his time with Gopi.

CHAPTER 8

AMAR

Gopi was two years older than me. He always made a point of reminding me when it came to making the decisions.

"Shall we go left or right?" he had asked me when we first met.

"Right?" I said.

"Let's go left," he said. "I'm two years older so I know best."

And that's how it was from that moment on.

I didn't know my mother or my father. All I know is that I was found as a baby on the doorstep of the temple by a priest who took pity on me.

The priest took me to his home and looked after me in his small house where the cracks in the walls were so wide I could poke my fingers through them. Lizards sunbathing on the flat roof would scurry away quickly whenever I tried to catch them. And I remember a constant bitter smell of *haldi* paste in the house from the Nataraja idol of the god Shiva, which was only faintly masked by a cloud of perfumed smoke rising from the burning incense sticks.

But that's all I remember of him. He died a few years later. I was four years old, maybe five, when his relatives came to pick apart their inheritance. It was made very clear I was no longer welcome. The Delhi pavement became my new home and I learned I had to grow up quickly to survive.

That first night sleeping rough I didn't sleep at all. Every sound made me jump and I remember crying for so long that I thought I would drown in my own tears. I wandered the streets for hours until I found myself at the train station. There, amongst the other street children, I curled up and shut my eyes, sleeping beside a group who were hidden away in a corner.

As soon as it was light, the children woke up, ready to work. They loitered by the busy parts of the station, their hands outstretched asking for money, and I learned by watching them. But commuters often walked on by, not even sparing me a glance, so instead I had to survive by eating scraps from the floor.

It was there that I met Eagle. He was an older child. He wore a hat with a feather in it and I remember thinking he was so glamorous as he smoked his cigarettes and spat out red globs of chewed *paan*, mixing the betel leaves with tobacco like an adult.

Eagle took me in. He fed me, gave me water and even gave me clothes and shoes to replace the ones I was fast growing out of. He took me to his place, a derelict mud-walled shack on the edge of the city where ten other street children lived too. Though now we weren't street children, we were Eagle's Children.

In exchange for a place to stay he expected me to bring him money. He taught me how to look pitiful, how to prey on the wives and friends of the British Raj, and how to sing the national anthem, because Eagle's Children weren't beggars. No, we were performers.

I was small for my age so my earning potential was great, he told me. Cute and small with the ability to sing the national anthem meant I could earn lots of money from wealthy members of the British Raj.

I mistook Eagle for a kind young man who took pity on a poor boy.

He was not kind.

He beat us daily. First with reeds and then with a stick if we didn't bring him enough money. And if we didn't bring him *any* money, he beat us harder. And if we cried, he beat us even harder again.

Eagle owned us. If we threatened to leave, he said he would kill us.

I was scared but I couldn't leave for fear of being killed. Every night I would plan my escape but by the morning I would lose my nerve, too frightened by Eagle and his punishments.

And then one day, he disappeared.

There were rumours amongst Eagle's Children that he had been killed by the people that owned *him* and to whom he owed even more money than we owed to Eagle. There was even a rumour that he had been welcomed into the circle of friends that surrounded the British Raj, but somehow I could not see his feathered hat and *paan*-chewing habit mixing with the rich men and their fat wallets.

With no Eagle, Eagle's Children had to fend for themselves. I had never been fully accepted into the group, so when they planned to take a train south in search of work, I wasn't surprised when they didn't ask me to join them. We parted ways and I headed back into the city, returning to my life as a street child.

That first night, I made my way back to the Gauri Shankar Temple, the only place I knew as home. I'd been lying down on the steps for maybe an hour, dozing in and out of sleep, because sleep was the only thing that took my mind off hunger, when a temple worker shooed me off the step with her broom.

"Shall we go left or right?" a voice asked.

I looked up to see a boy a few years older than me peering down.

"Right?" I said.

"Let's go left," he said. "I am older, so I know best."

I followed him without question. I still don't know why. Perhaps because he had the kindest face I had seen in a long while or perhaps because I really didn't have anywhere else to go.

Even though I remained hungry, homeless and cold, Gopi saved me. See, there are things worse than being hungry, or not having a home, or being cold.

There's loneliness.

With Gopi I was never alone. He too had been left to fend for himself on the streets. His mother had died in childbirth when he was born and his father, who had spent the family's money on alcohol and gambling, had never been able to look at Gopi without holding him responsible for her death. Gopi ran away from home at the age of four, hoping the streets would be kinder to him than his father, who never came looking for him.

Gopi and I would wake up before the whole of Delhi and lie in wait for the market stalls to open. Every tomato that fell was scooped up by Gopi, who was the master of turning his shirt into a basket, whilst I provided the distraction of being the lost young boy looking for his mother. And when that hustle ran its course, we would find a new part of Delhi to roost. Gopi was all the family I needed and soon my stomach started to ache from laughter instead of hunger.

We took on small jobs for *chai wallahs*, delivering teas to the businessmen who twirled their moustaches and talked about money. In exchange, the *chai wallahs* would give us tea and a snack to share at the end of the day.

Gopi taught me all about rich men and their fat wallets and how the fat wallets opened every time I called them "sir" when I delivered their tea.

The first time we had enough money, we bought ourselves two thick slices of melon and sucked the sweet fruit juice dry from the flesh like we were kings feasting at a banquet.

We would take our melon slices and try and sneak into the Regal Cinema to watch a film. It was Gopi's dream to save up enough money to visit our favourite actor, Ashok Kumar, and ask him to make us famous.

Those years were the best years of my life.

But then the talk of the British Raj leaving and the country being cut in two started.

Violence between gangs of Hindus, Sikhs and Muslims drove the rich men and their fat wallets out of Delhi. Gopi and I started to run out of places to hide and ways to make money. Even the *chai wallahs* stopped offering us work, choosing to deliver tea themselves.

Everyone was afraid and so were we. We thought so many times about leaving Delhi, but it was our home. For all her faults, her cracked pavements and cold nights, Delhi had given us a home, she'd given us food and she'd given us a family in each other.

Just after Independence Day, Gopi met a man who had some work for us down by the railway tracks. We were to be paid handsomely and Gopi was excited to earn some proper money so we could go and see Ashok Kumar.

"We will be the rich men with fat wallets," he said.

I woke up the next day with a raging fever. I could barely walk. Gopi said he would go to work and come back.

He never returned.

I searched for days at the train station, down by the tracks and through the streets, calling out his name and walking until my knees locked and I couldn't go on. He had disappeared completely.

A man told me of a riot in Sadar Bazaar and I remember collapsing to the ground, fearing the worst. I prayed to God that Gopi was safe. It was the first and last time I asked God for a favour.

I spent that day asking everyone if they had seen Gopi. No one remembered him apart from a potter who recalled a boy maybe two years older than me who had been caught up in the attack as he tried to escape.

I found Gopi's body in Sadar Bazaar later that day. He was piled amongst other bodies, lying in the gutter, ready to be shifted off the road, like a bag of rubbish.

India had given me my best friend and the partition had taken him away.

CHAPTER 9

IBRAHIM

Today was my twelfth birthday. It was the first I'd spent without my family.

Every year, since I could remember, I would wake up and find Ammi and Abbu walking around the house, doing the things they always did as though they had forgotten my birthday. It was a joke they played together. And when Nafia was born, I was roped in too.

We would start breakfast and I'd get my books for school. Nafia would wander out, full of smiles, holding her doll, and go straight to Abbu, who would shoo her away, telling her he was going to be late for work. Then she would go to Ammi and every time Nafia tried to say the words, "It's my birthday!" Ammi would stuff a handful of food into her mouth so she could never quite finish the sentence.

I would swing my school bag over my shoulder and say goodbye. Abbu and I would walk towards the door and just as Nafia's face fell and her eyes grew huge and wet with tears, we would whip round and shout, "Happy Birthday!" and Ammi would sing and scoop Nafia up in her arms.

Every year it was the same.

When I was eight, we took a trip to Dehradun for Ammi's birthday. I remember watching out of the car window at the land growing greener and lusher and the trees becoming bushier with leaves as we headed towards the mountains and the forest.

We stopped for a picnic and as Ammi fed Nafia, Abbu helped me build a kite. We used Abbu's newspaper and branches from a tree. Abbu used twine from our picnic parcels to tie the branches into a cross and loop the paper over.

I found long reeds to tie to the end of the kite so it would flutter in the wind, creating the sound of rain pattering down on a tin roof as the reeds struck the paper.

"Run further," Abbu shouted as I took the kite and ran fast into the wind.

I flung the kite over my head, and as it caught the breeze Abbu let out the rest of the twine. It tossed and turned over and over, swooping down and soaring back up as I chased it, leaping high to try and catch it.

The kite eventually flew into a tree, and as I sobbed into Ammi's *dupatta* she told me the tree had only wanted its branches back and that good boys who let trees have their branches back could get ice cream after dinner.

Abbu was a senior doctor and was one of only a few Indians selected to join the Dehradun Club. We were going to the club to celebrate Ammi's birthday. Ammi dressed me and Nafia in our finest clothes and she had bought us both shiny new shoes that squeaked when we walked. We were under strict instructions not to play in the grass in our new shoes and I took extra care to place one foot after the other on the ground so that dust from the road didn't scuff the shine.

We sat on the balcony of the club for Ammi's special birthday dinner. We ate off china plates with gold cutlery whilst wearing stiff napkins the size of sheets tucked into our clothes.

I remember there was music and dancing in the night and there had been an English lady in a long white dress who took my hands and spun me around to the music. I remember laughing so hard when Ammi and Abbu tried to imitate the British ladies and gentlemen dancing, looking awkward and stiff, arm in arm. Nafia slept soundly in the corner on the floor, but I did everything I could to stay awake and not miss a minute.

Treats, like trips to the Dehradun Club, only came as a result of me doing well at school and keeping out of trouble. I was expected to follow in Abbu's footsteps of course. I was to be a good son, a good big brother, a good Muslim and a good student. I had to go to school and stay at the top of my class throughout my education. I would then go on to a distinguished university in England and after graduating with a first-class honours degree, return to a job in India as a doctor or a barrister, before settling in the role of whatever the most senior position was. Just like Abbu.

Though I liked the idea of being invited into the exclusive Dehradun Club and dancing with English ladies in long white dresses, I secretly had another passion that I didn't dare share with Abbu.

From a young age, Ammi would sneak me out of school without telling Abbu, and we would go to watch the pictures. I learned most of my Hindi from watching films and not from actually being in class.

It was our special treat. Each week, Ammi and I would learn all the songs from the films and sing them at home. Ammi even started harmonium lessons so we could sing to music, and when I slept, my dreams would be choreographed to our singing.

The costumes, the music, the dancing – it all took me to another world where I could be free and escape Abbu's dreams of me in a senior job. It was all so breathtaking. I'd get lost in the stories and later I would tell all my friends about the latest exploits of our favourite film stars.

Abbu always wore a look of disappointment if I asked to go to the pictures at the weekend. He told me that the "frivolity of the cinema would rot my brain" and that I should focus on my studies instead.

I loved Abbu and I never wanted to disappoint him but I wanted to be like Ashok Kumar more than anything. He was effortless and suave and Ammi would swoon every time he showed up on screen.

Going to the Regal during school time remained our secret.

One time, Ammi even let me invite Faisal and Suleiman. When she dropped them home, they got in trouble with their mothers for skipping school. They were caned, and they showed me their long angry welts the next day. But we all agreed that it had been worth it as we sang 'Aaj Himalay Ki Choti Se', from the film *Kismet*, as we marched all the way home from school that day.

Ammi and I watched that film nearly thirty times that year, almost every week it showed in the cinema, until the huge painted posters came down to make way for the next film.

I had sung the song so many times that Nafia knew

it off by heart, despite having never seen the film. She asked me one day what the lyrics meant and I explained that they were telling the foreigners to keep their hands off India.

But in real life, the foreigners didn't keep their hands off India. And now I was being kicked out of the only country I'd ever known as home.

CHAPTER

10

AMAR

"You know, we should just use the money to find Ashok Kumar and ask him to fix the mess India is in," I joked.

"If anyone could stop the violence, it would be him," Ibrahim said.

"And he could turn us into film stars whilst he's at it," I said.

"Which one of Ashok Kumar's characters do you think I would be?" Ibrahim asked.

I jumped over a puddle and up on to a damp tree stump. "You would be the son of a doctor who is studying to be a doctor, of course. You would fall in love with a beautiful girl but be married off to someone else, heartbroken, and following your father's dream and not your own." I stood up and threw my hand up to my forehead, pretending to be anguished.

Ibrahim laughed, hopping up on to the tree stump in my place as I jumped down.

"What about me?" I grinned.

"You would be the loveable rogue pickpocket who could outwit the police," he declared. "You would be so scandalous, maybe too scandalous, and you would smoke cigarettes like the most scandalous of the rogue pickpockets," he said as he stroked his chin like a villain plotting his next move.

He jumped down and we kicked up the rainwater in the puddles.

"You know what I love the most about the cinema?" I said. "The sound of the projector. When that *tuk-tuk-tuk-tuk-tuk* sound starts, you know magic is going to happen."

"Yes!" Ibrahim said excitedly. "And when the light first hits the screen."

"And for a few hours, you can escape—" I stopped.

The image of Gopi at the Regal with his slice of melon flashed into my head. My chest felt tight. I couldn't help but feel guilty for enjoying my time with Ibrahim when Gopi was lying dead.

"You can escape your life," Ibrahim finished quietly.

I turned away from Ibrahim, tucking my hands deep into the pockets of my shirt. Ibrahim walked round to face me.

"I feel bad too," he said. "I feel like I'm not allowed to have fun or laugh because I don't know what has happened to Ammi and Abbu and Nafia."

I nodded. "Do you think your family is okay?"

Ibrahim looked down. "I don't know." He sighed. "I feel like I would know if something had happened to them. You know? Like deep in here," he said, tapping his chest. "Did you know when Gopi died?"

"I suppose so," I said, thinking back to that day. "I knew he wasn't back and that something had happened to him. I hoped it hadn't, but deep down I knew."

"I don't feel it. I don't feel that something bad has happened to them," Ibrahim said. "It's not just hope. I just really don't feel it."

"Good," I said, straightening up. "Then your family must be alive and we have to get you back to them."

We walked back towards the city centre, crossing the road whenever the track was too flooded on one side. As we got closer, crowds of people were hurrying alongside us in the same direction.

"What's going on?" Ibrahim asked as the crowd grew deeper and the chatter grew louder.

"I don't know," I had to shout over the commotion. I looked around for someone to ask and hurried to catch the lady in front of us.

"What's going on?" I asked her, running to keep up with her as she strode on ahead with her daughter.

"The prime minister is here!" she replied.

We followed the praising chants of "*Nehru Ki Jai*" as masses of people clapped and chanted, cheering for the prime minister. We were swallowed up by the throng of people, crying for joy as they shouted louder and louder. And then the man next to us bellowed, "There he is!"

Ibrahim pinched my arm and pointed towards the stage.

The raucous crowd quietened as Prime Minister Nehru, in his white *kurta* and jacket, stepped forward towards the microphone and spoke. He looked just like his picture in the newspapers. His voice boomed over our heads and seemed to reach out for miles.

I climbed up onto a broken wall and heaved Ibrahim up alongside me.

"Get up on my shoulders," Ibrahim said.

"But your arm—" I started.

"Just get on," he insisted, crouching down so I could climb up his back.

Up high on Ibrahim's wobbly shoulders, I could see faces for miles and miles. The crowd stretched so far back, and I could see Hindus, Muslims and Sikhs standing alongside one another.

The prime minister spoke to all of us. He spoke about the violence and how he wanted it to be over.

"This must be put down and suppressed," he said.

Ibrahim squeezed my leg as the prime minister talked about protecting Muslims on India's side of the border.

As Prime Minister Nehru continued to speak, it became difficult to hear his words over the rising sound of the crowd. People all around us were chatting feverishly and I even heard one woman tell her children that Gandhiji was coming to join the prime minister.

Gandhi? Gandhi was *here*? In Delhi?

I'd heard about Gandhiji from a *chai wallah*. He'd told me of a man named Gandhi who wanted a united India more than anything. He had been fighting for this but without weapons. The *chai wallah* told us of a time before either Gopi or I were born when the British Raj introduced a tax on salt. Gandhiji had walked more than two hundred miles to the sea to make his own salt from the seawater in protest of the tax. Thousands and thousands of people had joined the Salt March defying the Raj and the unjust taxes.

Gopi and I had mocked the *chai wallah* and his stories behind his back but we continued to hear more and more about Gandhi from the market vendors. Gandhiji wanted independence for India and he wanted a united India. He protested for India's independence with a hunger strike, showing the world that violence wasn't needed to make your voice heard. He even spent time in jail, all in the name of peace in India, and now the revered elderly man had the ear of the prime minister. Gopi had believed that if anyone could save India it was Gandhiji. He had always said we should travel to meet him once we had saved up enough money.

If Gandhi was in my home city, I had to try and see him for Gopi.

But as I looked around at the sea of people below me, I started to have a sinking feeling in my stomach.

"I've heard of Gandhi," Ibrahim shouted to me excitedly over the noise of the crowd. "Abbu told me he has been protesting for India's freedom for years. Do you really think he'll come?"

As the prime minister left the stage, chants of "*Nehru Ki Jai*" started up again. This was the India I wanted. This was the India where Gopi would still be alive and we would still be sneaking into the Regal to watch films.

But this wasn't the India we lived in. I looked down at Ibrahim, who was beaming up at me.

The prime minister's talk had been just that. Talk.

India had been burning down for a long while before the partition and what had Prime Minister Nehru done then?

Now he was pleading with people who had no qualms about picking up something sharp and slashing their previous good neighbours' necks with it. The violence was only getting worse. There were no solutions. There never were. I'd learned that early on. The night would come and the mobs would be out.

Ibrahim grinned up at me, inspired by the prime minister's words, ready to take on the world and find his family.

I had to get him out of Delhi. I had lost one brother already. I didn't want to lose another.

CHAPTER 11

IBRAHIM

"We have to go now," Amar said, sliding down my back.

He reached out a hand and took mine to help me down from the wall.

"Now," he insisted.

The crowd was chanting and it felt like I was back at Independence Day when the Muslims, Hindus and Sikhs were united in their celebrations together and we ate *mithai* in the streets.

"Why?" I asked Amar. "I want to stay and hear Gandhi speak to the people."

My heart fell as I saw the sour look on his face darken further. I understood he was doing me a favour by protecting me and that he was devastated by the death of his friend but he really needed to lighten up.

So I told him so.

"I need to lighten up?" he questioned, pulling me out of the crowd. "You need to *grow* up. And quickly."

"What *is* your problem?"

"My problem is that the mobs will be out soon and you'll be in danger," he said, dragging me further away.

I yanked my arm from his grasp and he stopped, turning hard to face me. "We aren't in danger, Amar!" I exclaimed. I pointed to the crowd still chanting together for the prime minister and Gandhi. "Can't you see all these people want peace?"

"And what about the ones who don't?" he challenged.

"What about them?" I said, shielding my eyes with the crook of my hand and pretending to look around for signs of danger. "I don't see them anywhere."

He looked hurt and for a moment I readied myself to apologize.

"Come on, we have to go," he insisted again.

I pressed my lips together and gave him a hard smile. "Stop rushing, Amar," I said, holding on to him. "Can't you just enjoy this moment of peace? I know your friend is dead but we don't have to be miserable all the time."

I immediately regretted what I'd said and wished I could grab those words back as they hung in the air between us.

He lurched at me, glowering. "How protected were you, Maharaja?" he taunted, his nostrils flaring. "You must've seen the violence growing over the past year." He looked me up and down like I was the dirt on the back of his slippers. "For all your book smarts, you know nothing. There will never be peace. Your kind and my kind have never got on."

I stumbled back. His words landed like a punch to my gut. "My parents may have protected me from the truth," I retorted. "And I may be naïve. But I know enough to know that there is no 'your kind' and no 'my kind'. There is just us. We are both Indians."

"Well, you're a Pakistani now," he said.

"I was born here in India, just like you," I said, unable to stop my voice from rising and the hot tears springing up in my eyes.

"Well then you don't need my help finding the border because you are clearly in the right country already." He stormed off, walking faster and faster, until he was running, dodging hordes of people, and I could no longer see him.

I wiped my tears and looked around. I wasn't sure where I was. I didn't know Delhi the way Amar did, but I didn't need him. I could look after myself.

I turned and walked towards what looked like a row of market stalls. I was pretty sure I recognized them.

I didn't need Amar. He was constantly looking for problems, hanging over me like a black cloud. I'd been through enough already and I needed to stay positive for Ammi, Abbu and Nafia.

And now I was on my own, I didn't need to pay Amar. I was going to buy myself the biggest plate of food and eat it all by myself.

As I turned the corner, I bumped into a group of men. Without thinking, I quickly apologized in

Urdu, instead of speaking Hindi like Amar had told me. Realizing my mistake, I was about to step back out to the main road I'd come off when a rough hand grabbed a clump of my hair and pulled me forwards.

"You speak Urdu?" the man holding my head snarled at me. "Sounds like we have a little Muslim here,"

"I . . . I . . ."

"Muslim scum dressed up as a good Hindu boy, eh?" he mocked.

I opened my mouth to scream but nothing came out.

The man let go of my hair and grabbed me by the face, his thick, coarse hand closing tight over my mouth. He raised up his other hand.

He was holding an iron bar.

He pushed it against my head, grinding it slowly into my skin, until it felt like it would pierce my skull and the sticky ooze of blood would burst through.

"I'm going to enjoy this," he sneered, grinding the bar further into my head.

I screamed out into his hand as a sharp hot pain burned through my skull.

"Leave him alone!"

Amar was behind him, holding up his catapult armed with a rock.

The man smirked at him. “What do you want, little hero?”

“He’s mine,” Amar said defiantly.

“What?” the man said, confused.

“He’s mine,” Amar said again. “I’ve been keeping him to torture for the death of my friend.” He drew back the elastic on his catapult further.

My heart dropped to my stomach and the sky started to spin. Amar was supposed to be my friend. I thought he was my brother.

The man laughed and his *paan*-stained teeth glinted in the sun. He gripped my face hard and hurled me to the floor. I screamed out as my shoulder hit the ground hard.

“He’s all yours,” the man barked, swinging the iron bar in his hand and stepping back to allow Amar through.

Amar strode towards me and lurched over with his catapult aimed squarely at my face.

“Please, Amar—”

“Quiet!” he shouted at me.

The man stood there, unmoving.

Amar turned to him slowly. "Leave us," he said.

"Why should I?" the man asked. "I want to see this one squashed into the ground."

"He has money," Amar said. "You can have it all if you leave us."

"What?" I said.

"Give it to him," Amar instructed.

"Why are you doing this, Amar?" I asked.

"Give it to him," Amar said again, through gritted teeth.

I reached to my pocket and unpinned it, pulling out a small wedge of the cash.

"All of it," the man snapped.

I pulled the entire roll out and threw it towards the man. He picked it up and counted through the notes, whistling in admiration. He looked at Amar, shrugged and shot me a grin before turning and leaving the yard.

It was just me and Amar now. He was still standing over me, his catapult ready to launch with a huge sharpened rock in the slingshot.

"Please don't do this, Amar," I begged.

CHAPTER 12

AMAR

"Get up," I said, grabbing Ibrahim hard and pulling him to his feet.

"Please, Amar," he pleaded.

"Get. Up."

Ibrahim stumbled to his feet, pressing his hand against his head tight. Blood oozed through his fingers where the iron bar had split his skin wide open like an overripe mango.

"We have to get you out of here," I hissed.

I pulled him close, shielding him, as we headed out of the yard. His face was ashen and his chin trembled as he whimpered.

"You're . . . you're not going to kill me?" he asked hesitantly.

"Of course not!" I scoffed. "You're my brother now, Ibrahim," I scolded him. "Besides, if I was going to kill you, I would've thrown you off the clock tower so I wouldn't have to share the mangoes with you."

He gawped at me, scared.

"It's a joke," I said. "*You* need to lighten up."

We turned out of the yard when I heard the man with the iron bar.

"HEY! GET BACK HERE!" he yelled.

"We need to run," I said to Ibrahim. "Now!"

Our feet pounded the ground, kicking up rain as we ran fast. We sprinted hard, dodging people and jumping walls. Heavy clouds loomed overhead, turning the streets dark. The rain started to lash down again. Our legs churned harder and harder but we never stopped once, not even to look back in case the man was still close behind.

We careered into Pul Bangash. Ibrahim's breath was heavy and rasping. People appeared in the doorways of their homes looking for danger as we ran past, as though we were a sign of a mob heading their way. Mothers looked frightened as they pulled their children back, shielding them behind their *dupattas*. Ibrahim collapsed to the ground and I picked him up, carrying him towards a sheltered doorway, dragging his feet along the floor, as the rain soaked us both through.

His breathing was ragged and he was shivering. I hugged him close, rubbing his shoulders, transferring what heat I could to him.

He began to sob, wailing as tears ran down his cheeks alongside the raindrops and into the blood that dripped down the side of his head. He screamed out as I held him tight.

He needed to be back with his family. *I* needed to get him back to his family.

"I can't believe you came back for me," he whispered into my chest.

"It's okay," I said.

"Thank you . . . brother," he said, pulling away and looking up at me.

His sobs quietened to dry heaves as I held him tighter.

A pain built in the back of my throat. I should never have left him. He should never have been in the yard with the man with the iron bar.

"I'm sorry we argued," I said.

"No," Ibrahim said, sitting up. "I'm sorry for what I said about Gopi. I wish I could take back my words."

"It's okay," I said.

"No, it's not," he said remorsefully. "You have been nothing but kind to me. You have been a good friend to me."

"And you have been a good friend to me too," I said, because he had. I never thought I would laugh again after Gopi died and Ibrahim had shown me how.

We sat for a moment in our soaked *kurtas*, looking out as sheets of rain obscured the street. Torrents of water gushed down the road, deafening and wild.

And almost as suddenly as it had started, the rain stopped.

"I can't believe you gave him all your money," Ibrahim said, breaking the silence.

"I know! I hope that greedy oaf gets pickpocketed on his way home."

Ibrahim tutted. "I can still taste his hand in my mouth," he said, spitting to one side. He looked at his empty turned-out pocket. "I don't have anything to pay you with when we get to the border, Amar."

I shook my head. "Don't worry. It's not important."

"You really are a good friend," he said with a smile.

He was my friend so I had to be honest with him. "I can't take you to the border, Ibrahim." I looked down, unable to meet his eye as I confessed I had to let him down. "You're injured and tired and cold and we don't have any supplies," I said. "And even if you weren't injured, I don't entirely know where to go. It wouldn't be safe for either of us."

Ibrahim's face fell.

"Don't worry," I reassured him. "I can take you somewhere where you can get out of Delhi safely."

"Where?" he asked.

"I overheard some women talking about selling *chana*," I said. "They were heading to Purana Qila because there is a refugee camp for Muslims there. The Muslim League even has their own guard to protect you. You can get safely out of Delhi with their help."

He nodded.

"Are you okay to walk?" I asked. "We should leave now before it gets dark."

He grimaced but nodded again and I helped him to his feet.

We walked towards Sadar Bazaar. Before the violence, this had been a neighbourhood where Muslims and Hindus lived side by side, but now I could see they lived on opposite sides of the road.

We headed on through the deserted streets of Charkhiwalan Gali, walking slowly as Ibrahim leaned on me for support. As we came closer to the camp, we were joined by a group of refugees heading in the same direction. We continued on silently as the group grew larger, some travelling as families, some alone, some with belongings, some with only the shirts they wore, all heading towards the refugee camp at Purana Qila. A woman carried two babies, her feet swollen and cut, her babies' wailing the only sound alongside the slap of feet in dirt as we all trudged along the street.

Ibrahim and I ducked away from the group when his breathing grew heavy again. His head was still bleeding. I tore a piece of fabric from his sling and tied it around his head to help stop the bleeding.

"Let's go," Ibrahim insisted, leaning into me as we got to our feet.

Within a few hours we had reached Purana Qila. We were exhausted and shivering from the rain. We stopped short of the camp, allowing others to pass. I had a couple of rupees in my pocket and managed to buy us both a *roti* each.

We sat down and devoured them in silence as a voice boomed over a loudspeaker within the Purana Qila walls announcing a train would be leaving for Pakistan shortly from Pragati Maidan station.

"It's nearby," I said, pointing in the direction of the station.

Neither of us said one word as we sat watching the stream of refugees enter the camp. Once Ibrahim was on the other side of those walls, we would never see each other again. He would be a Pakistani and I would remain an Indian. Our friendship would be over because of a border neither of us asked for.

Ibrahim sat up straight and then stood up, brushing down his *kurta* and adjusting his sling. He straightened up the bandage on his head. He was ready to make his way into the camp. My stomach churned. I wasn't ready to say goodbye.

I looked down and noticed my feet. I smiled, thinking back to the morning we had met.

"Do you want your shoes back?" I asked.

Ibrahim shook his head. "You keep them," he said. "You'll need nice shoes for when you meet Ashok Kumar some day."

He grabbed me, pulling me up, and hugged me hard.

"Thank you for everything," he said, his voice muffled by my shoulder.

"Please look after yourself, brother," I choked.

"You too, brother," he said.

And then he left.

EPILOGUE

AMAR

I never heard from Ibrahim again.

Every now and then I thought I caught a glimpse of him in the crowds at Chandni Chowk but I would rush over to find it wasn't him. Sometimes I thought I heard him call my name but I would turn to find no one there.

I often wondered if Ibrahim had made it across the border safely. I wondered if he had managed to find his family. I liked to think he was watching films with his Ammi again. And that he told his sister stories of the time his friend Amar took him to eat the best mangoes in Delhi.

Life on the streets was hard, but I managed to stay safe and take care of myself. A *chai wallah* took pity on me and offered me work. He didn't pay me but he let me drink the leftover dregs of tea at the end of the day if I did a good job and stayed out of his way.

I went back to sleeping at the temple but Delhi didn't feel like home any more, without Gopi. And without Ibrahim. The city had changed. I had lost a lot – family, friends – but I knew I wasn't the only one to suffer.

A few weeks after I left Ibrahim at Purana Qila, I heard of a vicious attack on a Pakistan Special leaving Delhi. The train had been full of Muslim refugees trying to get across the border to safety.

There were no survivors.

AUTHOR'S NOTE

In the aftermath of India's independence from British rule in 1947, British India was split into Pakistan and India. Hindus and Sikhs were to live in India and Muslims were to live in Pakistan.

Despite centuries of Hindus, Muslims and Sikhs living for the most part peacefully alongside each other, this division forced underlying tensions between the different religious groups to the surface.

The partition led to what is still considered one of the largest and deadliest mass migrations as Muslims crossed the border to Pakistan and Hindus and Sikhs crossed to India. It is suggested that more than fourteen million people were uprooted from their homes and at least a million people died as violence tore across the two newly formed countries.

Carnage became commonplace and many had to

leave quickly, giving up their homes and possessions and often leaving behind their neighbours and friends. Trains full of those trying to flee across the border were attacked by both sides, with entire carriages full of massacred refugees arriving at station platforms in India and Pakistan with the messages "A present from Pakistan" and "A present from India" scrawled on the side of the carriages.

Over seventy years later, the horrors of what went on still haunt those who survived.

But many wanted peace, and leaders such as Gandhi led non-violent rallies to call an end to the violence. In researching this book, I was astounded by the power of the human spirit and its ability to rebuild during adversity. The partition saw many stories of Hindus, Muslims and Sikhs helping each other out and protecting one another. And not just friends and neighbours rallying together but strangers too, risking their own lives to do so. There are stories of kindness and forgiveness. There are stories of lives being rebuilt and families being reunited. For the millions affected by the partition, there is an individual story for each and every one of them.

Religious tension still exists today. In fact, tension exists between many different groups, be it different races, different sexualities or different socioeconomic groups around the world. Walls and borders are created and violence is all too easily seen as a solution.

I hope that in learning from stories of the past, we can look beyond what divides us and see that we have more in common than we do differences. Just like Ibrahim and Amar.

TIMELINE

1858 The British Indian Empire is established.
1877 Queen Victoria claims the title the Empress of India.
1885 The Indian National Congress is formed in an effort to gain independence for India.
1920 Mahatma Gandhi begins his campaign of non-violent protest against the British government.
1947 In August, India wins its independence from the British and splits into two states, India and Pakitstan. The Muslim state of Pakistan is established in the north. The partition of India forces millions of people to leave their homes. Jawaharlal Nehru becomes the first prime minister of India.
1948 War breaks out between India and Pakistan over the border land of Kashmir.

THE PEOPLE

JAWAHARLAL NEHRU: an Indian independence activist and the first prime minister of India (1947–64)

MAHATMA GANDHI: a great civil rights leader from India. He believed in non-violent, peaceful protests.

GLOSSARY

'AAJ HIMALAY KI CHOTI SE': this is a song from the film *Kismet*, considered to be patriotic by Indians

ASHOKA CHAKRA: the blue wheel at the centre of the Indian flag

BRITISH RAJ: when the British had control over India from 1858 to 1947

CHANA: chickpeas

CHANDNI CHOWK: one of the oldest and busiest markets in the city of Delhi

DAAL: lentils

DIWALI: is the Hindu 'festival of lights' which celebrates the New Year

DIYA: a small oil lamp

DUPATTA: a long scarf often worn with a *salwar kameez*

EID: Eid al-Fitr is a Muslim holiday celebrated when Ramadan, the month of fasting, finishes.

HALDI: turmeric

HINDI: a language native to India and commonly spoken by Hindus

HINDU: a follower of Hinduism, one of the oldest religions in the world

JAMA MASJID: located in Delhi, Jama Masjid is one of the largest mosques in India

KISMET: the title of a 1943 film starring Ashok Kumar.

The word 'kismet' means fate.

KURTA: a long-sleeved long shirt worn with trousers

LATHI: a stick used as a weapon, usually by the police

MITHAI: Indian sweets

MUSLIM: a follower of Islam

MUSLIM LEAGUE: a political party established in 1906. The party played an important role in the creation of Pakistan as a Muslim state.

NATARAJA: the dancing form of the Hindu god Lord Shiva

'NEHRU KI JAI': Hindi for 'victory to Nehru'

PAAN: betel leaves that are chewed with betel nuts or tobacco

ROTI: a flat circular bread

RUPEE: currency used in India and Pakistan

SALWAR KAMEEZ: a traditional outfit of loose trousers with a tunic top

SARI: a long length of fabric worn wrapped around the waist and draped over the body

SIKH: a follower of Sikhism

SIKHISM: a religion founded in Punjab in northern India

SHIVA: the Hindu god of destruction

TOPI: a circular prayer hat worn by Muslims

URDU: the official national language of Pakistan, commonly spoken by Pakistani Muslims